Festivals of the World

JAPAN

Gareth Stevens Publishing
MILWAUKEE

Written by
SUSAN MCKAY

Designed by
JAILANI BASARI

Picture research by
SUSAN JANE MANUEL

First published in North America in 1997 by
Gareth Stevens Publishing
1555 North RiverCenter Drive, Suite 201
Milwaukee, Wisconsin 53212 USA

For a free color catalog describing Gareth Stevens'
list of high-quality books and multimedia programs,
call
1-800-542-2595 (USA)
or 1-800-461-9120 (Canada).
Gareth Stevens Publishing's Fax: (414) 225-0377.

© **TIMES EDITIONS PTE LTD 1997**
REPRINTED 2000
Originated and designed by
Times Books International
an imprint of Times Editions Pte Ltd
Times Centre, 1 New Industrial Road
Singapore 536196
Printed in Malaysia

Library of Congress Cataloging-in-Publication Data:
McKay, Susan, 1972–
Japan / by Susan McKay.
p. cm. -- (Festivals of the world)
Includes bibliographical references and index.
Summary: Describes how the culture of Japan is
reflected in its festivals, including the Gion Festival,
the Fire Festivals, and the Sapporo Snow Festival.
ISBN 0-8368-1935-7 (lib. bdg.)
1.Festivals--Japan--Juvenile literature. 2 Japan--
Social life and customs--Juvenile literature. [1.
Festivals--Japan. 2. Japan--Social life and customs.]
I. Title. II. Series.
GT4884.A2M43 1997
394.26952--dc21   97-9114

2 3 4 5 6 7 8 9 04 03 02 01 00

CONTENTS

It's Festival Time . . .

The Japanese word for festival is *matsuri* [MAT-soo-ree]. There are matsuri celebrating everything from freeing insects to chasing wild horses.

Many Japanese festivals are based on events in history. Others are based on religion or superstition. But no matter where they come from, matsuri are always a time to enjoy. So, come along and walk over hot coals, dress as a samurai, and build a snow statue. It's festival time in Japan . . .

WHERE'S JAPAN?

Japan is a small group of islands lying between the Pacific Ocean and the Sea of Japan. There are four main islands in the archipelago: Honshu, Shikoku, Hokkaido, and Kyushu. Most people live on the main island, Honshu. The capital of Japan is Tokyo.

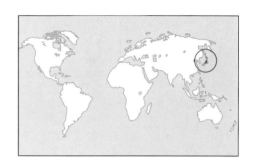

Who are the Japanese?

The **Ainu** [EYE-new] were the first settlers of the islands. They are believed to have come to Japan from Siberia. They are tall people with fair skin and wavy hair. The other early settlers of Japan came mostly from China, Korea, Malaya, and the South Pacific islands. They are usually shorter than the Ainu, and have darker skin and straight black hair.

A young Japanese boy dressed in formal clothes.

Over the centuries, the two groups began to fight, and eventually the smaller number of Ainu settlers were driven to the northernmost island of Hokkaido. Today, there are very few Ainu remaining, and their numbers are rapidly decreasing. The majority of Japanese are descendants of the migrants from China and Korea.

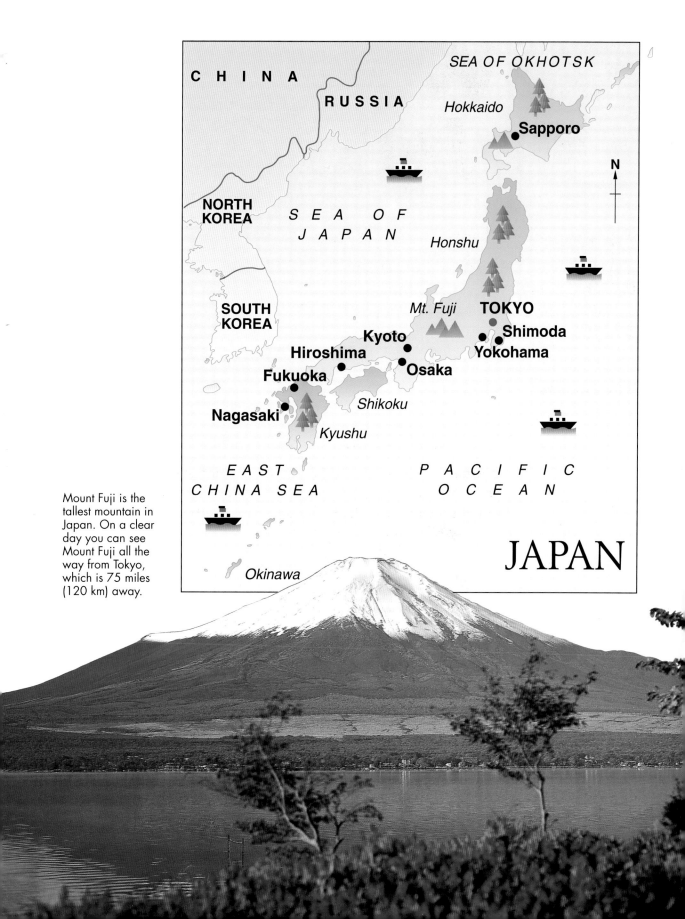

CHINA

RUSSIA

SEA OF OKHOTSK

Hokkaido

Sapporo

SEA OF JAPAN

NORTH KOREA

Honshu

SOUTH KOREA

N

Mt. Fuji

TOKYO

Shimoda

Kyoto

Yokohama

Hiroshima

Osaka

Fukuoka

Shikoku

Nagasaki

Kyushu

EAST CHINA SEA

PACIFIC OCEAN

Mount Fuji is the tallest mountain in Japan. On a clear day you can see Mount Fuji all the way from Tokyo, which is 75 miles (120 km) away.

Okinawa

JAPAN

WHEN'S THE MATSURI?

SPRING

- ✪ **GIRL'S DAY** ✪ **BUDDHA'S BIRTHDAY** ✪ **SETSUBUN**
- ✪ **AOI FESTIVAL**—An imperial procession of people dressed in clothes from the Heian period (8th–12th century).
- ✪ **MARCH OF THE SAMURAI**
- ✪ **BOY'S DAY** ✪ **BLACK SHIP FESTIVAL**—Celebrates Commodore Perry's landing at Shimoda in 1854. On this day there is a U.S. naval parade.
- ✪ **PEACE FESTIVAL**—Children all over Japan make paper cranes and send them to Hiroshima to decorate the peace monument.

SUMMER

- ✪ **GION FESTIVAL**
- ✪ **WILD HORSE FESTIVAL**—A Japanese rodeo is put on to honor the spirit of the samurai. People dress in traditional samurai uniforms from centuries ago.
- ✪ **OBON**—People welcome the spirits of their dead ancestors back into the home with huge feasts and special family celebrations.
- ✪ **TANABATA**—Bamboo cuttings are set up in houses and decorated with romantic poems to celebrate the one day of the year when the weaver girl and the cowherd stars can cross the Milky Way and meet.
- ✪ **DAIMONJI BONFIRE**

AUTUMN

- ✪ **SHICHI-GO-SAN**
- ✪ **ROUGH-HOUSE FESTIVAL**—Palanquins are carried to the shrine where they perform for the gods, competing against other palanquins.
- ✪ **KURAMA FIRE FESTIVAL**
- ✪ **DEMON DANCE**—Villagers present seven plays about hell.

WINTER

- ✪ **NEW YEAR**—The house is cleaned and decorated in preparation for the New Year. Temple bells are rung 108 times to mark the end of the old year and the beginning of the new.
- ✪ **NANAKUSA**—The seventh day of the New Year when all decorations are taken down and burned or thrown into the river as a form of purification.
- ✪ **SAPPORO SNOW FESTIVAL** ✪ **KAMAKURA FESTIVAL**
- ✪ **SEIJINSHIKI**—Coming of Age Day, when girls and boys celebrate turning 20 years old.
- ✪ **NAMAHAGE**—People dress up as monsters to scare children into being good in the coming year.

Heave-ho, heave-ho! Get into the fighting spirit for the Rough-House Festival.

GION FESTIVAL

I n mid-July, the city of Kyoto comes alive with the reawakening of hundreds of years of history. Kyoto is the ancient capital of Japan, so it is a special place for the Japanese. Thousands of people from across the country come to Kyoto and take to the streets to celebrate the Gion Festival.

Every year, one boy is chosen to be the festival's page boy.

Listen to a story…

In the year 869, a terrible disease swept the city of Kyoto. The emperor was concerned about his people, so he prayed to the gods for mercy. He went to Gion Shrine and made an offering of 66 halberds (spears with long handles and blades like axes), one for each of his provinces. Soon after, the disease disappeared and the city was saved. The emperor was so pleased he organized a huge parade. The floats made for the parade were called *hoko* [HO-ko].

Musicians surround the page boy at the top of the hoko.

8

What are hoko?

Hoko are huge boxes that weigh as much as 10 tons and measure as high as four stories. Because they are so big, the hoko have to be put together about 10 days before the festival. Each of the corners is supported by a wheel that measures about 8 feet (2.5 m) across. At the top of the box is a long pole that represents a halberd. The name of the hoko is determined by what is attached to the tip of the pole. If it is a half moon, for example, the hoko will be called the half moon hoko.

The page boy

Every year, one lucky boy is chosen to be the festival's page boy. He dresses in the robe and hat of a priest, and paints his face completely white. While all the floats are being put together for the parade, the page boy walks around and keeps an eye on the progress. All day long he is followed by an attendant who holds an umbrella over his head to keep the hot sun off him. The boy's family also gets to join in the excitement by dressing up in special costumes.

The night before the procession, paper lanterns are lit and strung throughout the city. The Yasaka Shrine below is the same shrine where the emperor prayed to the gods.

The procession

When the day of the procession finally arrives, everyone is very excited. People have traveled from across Japan to be in Kyoto on this day. Many people have put in a lot of effort to make sure all is ready.

A priest purifies the hoko by pouring salt over the wheels. The page boy takes his place of honor in a seat at the top of the hoko. From there he can watch the procession and the people in the streets below him.

Young men dressed in short coats and straw hats are the crew of the hoko. When they get the signal, they start to pull on the long rope attached to the box. Slowly it begins to move. It will take many men to pull the hoko through the streets because it is so heavy, and the wooden wheels are not meant to be steered.

Older men dressed in ancient court costumes lead the march. More men climb on top of the hoko. Their sleeves are filled with *chimaki* [CHEE-ma-kee], straw wrapped in bamboo leaves. These are good luck charms. As the hoko makes its way through the streets, the men throw the charms to the crowd. Hundreds of people line the streets to watch the procession.

Dressed in ancient court clothes for the Gion Festival.

Opposite: Pulling the hoko is no easy job as you can tell from the strained expression on these men's faces.

10

This girl is resting after the long procession. When the sun goes down, she will light her lantern.

Think about this

Kyoto is often called the "heart of old Japan" because it was the home of the imperial court for 1,100 years. You can still see palaces in Kyoto today. Can you think of any other countries that have moved their capital from one city to another?

Ready for next year

By the end of the day, the hoko crew are very tired. Boys from the crowd rush toward the hoko so they can help pull, too. The procession ends when the hoko finally reach their starting point again. After a rest, each hoko is taken apart and stored away until next year. The panels must be handled with great care because many of them are hundreds of years old. They are considered works of art because of the intricate patterns and designs.

CHILDREN'S FESTIVALS

I t is wonderful to be a child in Japan because there are so many holidays to celebrate childhood. There are special days for girls, boys, and for children aged seven, five, and three. Usually, Japanese children wear Western clothes, but during children's festivals, boys and girls dress in their best **kimono** [kee-MO-no].

Shichi-Go-San

Shichi-Go-San falls on the 15th of November. The name of the festival means "Seven-Five-Three." It is called Shichi-Go-San because the festival honors children of those ages. The Japanese believe that the ages seven, five, and three are so unlucky that any child is fortunate just to survive them.

The day usually begins with a visit to the shrine. Parents pray to the gods to give their children health and happiness. Vendors outside the shrine sell candy wrapped in a long, brightly colored bag. The candy is said to bring good luck and long life to those who eat it. Children have parties, receive presents, and are generally spoiled on this day.

Boys wear kimono, too. Only they wear theirs with wide, pleated pants called **hakama** [HA-ka-ma].

Opposite: This seven-year-old is dressed in her best kimono for Shichi-Go-San.

Boy's Day

This day is also known as the Iris Festival or Children's Day, but it really belongs to boys. On the morning of May 5th, the whole family takes a special bath, called Shobu-ya. The bath is said to wash away any bad luck. If iris leaves, *shobu* [SHO-boo] in Japanese, are put in the bath water, the boy will become strong and brave.

In front of the house, you can see another symbol of strength and courage—the carp. A few days before May 5th, cloth carp are hung from bamboo poles. The windsocks are flown throughout the holiday. There is a carp for each son. The largest fish, at the top of the pole, is for the eldest son. The smaller ones below are for his younger brothers.

Carp must fight their way upstream to lay their eggs. This is why they represent strength.

Folktales and warriors

In nearly every Japanese home, there is an alcove where scrolls hang to mark a special holiday. On Boy's Day, families decorate the alcove with toy weapons and famous warriors wearing traditional armor. Many of the warriors are well-known figures in Japanese history or folktales, such as Kintaro, the Golden Boy, and Momotaro, the Peach Boy who battled against the wicked giants.

Japanese boys hope to grow up as strong and brave as warriors.

14

Girl's Day

When March comes around there is an air of excitement in homes with daughters. Small boxes that have been stored all year are opened again. Inside them are dolls called **hina** [HEE-na]. The set of dolls is a special collection gathered by the family, sometimes over many years. The set includes a prince, a princess, ladies-in-waiting, a minister of state, court musicians, and courtiers.

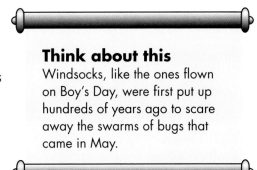

Think about this

Windsocks, like the ones flown on Boy's Day, were first put up hundreds of years ago to scare away the swarms of bugs that came in May.

How did the festival begin?

Long ago, Girl's Day marked the beginning of spring. In those days, people rubbed themselves with paper dolls to get rid of winter's evil spirits. Then they threw the dolls into the river to be carried away. Over time, sculptors began to make clay dolls. The dolls were so beautiful that no one wanted to throw them away. Soon the tiny figures were kept year after year as a set. Today, girls are told that March 3rd is a lucky day to get married.

These two are all set for their Girl's Day celebration.

FIRE FESTIVALS

any years ago, Japanese houses were made of wood and paper. Fire was both feared and revered because one tiny spark could set a whole village ablaze and leave thousands homeless.

According to the Japanese religion, Shinto, fire is purifying and can protect people from evil spirits. Fire is honored by the Japanese at the many fire festivals that take place throughout the country.

Above: Receiving a blessing from the priest before the ceremony.

Fire-walking ceremonies

Every year in August and September, Shinto priests and devotees take part in a fire-walking ceremony. Branches of firewood are bundled together and used to light a bed of coals. The priests walk around the coal beds until they have worked themselves into a trance-like state. Then, they throw a handful of salt onto the coals, rub salt on the bottoms of their feet, and walk slowly and calmly over the coals to the other side.

The reason the priests perform this ceremony every year is to prove to people that fire can be controlled. Throughout the ceremony, the priests murmur prayers. The prayers are believed to help them conquer the fire.

Kurama Fire Festival

Mount Wakakusa is the site of a grass-burning ceremony every year. This is to commemorate the friendly rivalry between two temples. The day ends with a huge fireworks display.

In the village of Kurama, another fire festival takes place every year. The highlight is a procession led by young boys. Men wearing short cotton coats follow behind them. All the marchers hold flaming baskets of branches high up in the air. The flames begin to grow higher and sparks fly through the air, but no one is scared because fire protects people from evil spirits.

Think about this

Shinto is a religion that is unique to Japan. In English *Shinto* means "way of the gods." Shintoists believe that spirits live in rocks, in the wind, in the sea, and in all parts of nature. These beliefs are an important part of many festivals and ceremonies in Japan.

Some people try to catch the sparks because they believe it will bring them good luck.

The fire gods

Bonfires line the main street of this tiny village. The parade goes up and down the street until the younger torchbearers grow tired and are taken to bed. Shortly before midnight, the crowd gathers and heads toward the village shrine. When they have reached the shrine, the Shinto priest whispers a farewell prayer, and the fire gods leave the village until next year.

MARCH OF THE SAMURAI

There is a saying in Japan that goes "Never say *kekko* [KE-ko] until you have seen Nikko." Kekko means "magnificent," and Nikko is the beautiful town where the March of the Samurai takes place every year on May 17th and 18th.

Listen to a story…

Starting in the 12th century, the emperor of Japan was locked away in his palace while a military dictator, called **shogun** (SHO-goon], ruled the country. The shogun kept his power through his special army of warriors, called samurai.

In 1616, a very powerful shogun died. His grandson decided to build a fantastic shrine decorated with carvings and sheets of gold in his honor. On the day that his body was moved to the shrine, there was a huge procession of all the samurai in the shogun's army.

Every year, the March of the Samurai recreates the scene that first took place in 1616.

Shinto priests play an important role in the festival.

The One Thousand Person Procession

A Shinto priest on horseback leads the procession through the streets to the shrine. Behind him come the townspeople, wearing the dress of storekeepers, artists, performers, and of course warriors from hundreds of years ago.

Musicians march along with the procession, providing entertainment.

One group of strong, young men is in charge of carrying the **palanquin**. It is said to hold the spirit of the shogun who died in 1616. Although his body is still buried in the shrine, some people like to pretend that he is being carried to his resting place again, just as he was many years ago.

A Shinto priest shades himself from the sun with a parasol.

It takes many strong men to lift the palanquin because it is very heavy.

Samurai

The samurai of Japan were a lot like the knights of medieval Europe. They were great warriors who were not afraid to die for their lord. They always carried two swords. They were very experienced in fencing, wrestling, archery, and horsemanship. In battle, they wore fantastically-shaped helmets and heavy armor made of metal strips held together with leather and cord.

During the procession, you can see people dressed as samurai from the 17th and 18th centuries. Some carry only a bow and arrow. Others carry swords and spears. Still others carry matchlock guns that were introduced to Japan by the Portuguese in the 16th century.

These two samurai are taking their role very seriously.

Children also get to take part in the procession.

Think about this
The name of the shogun who is commemorated in Nikko each year is Tokugawa Ieyasu. Today, he is considered one of the greatest and bravest warriors of all time.

Archers carry special bows and arrows to compete in yabusame.

Yabusame

There is a fantastic contest to end the day. It is a contest that tests the skill of archers on horseback. It is called **yabusame** [ya-boo-SA-may], and it was one of the favorite sports of the samurai.

Six small, square targets are attached to a fence that surrounds the playing ground. The rider has to race down the course toward the first three targets at a full gallop and try to hit these targets as he passes them. Then he must quickly turn around and ride back the other way to hit the three targets at the other end. It takes a bowman with great skill to hit all six targets.

SNOW FESTIVAL

I n most of Japan there is not much snow in winter. But in the northern city of Sapporo, there is heavy snowfall. That's why every year, on the second Thursday of February, the Sapporo Snow Festival is held. The city's main square becomes a showcase for ice sculptures and snow statues, some of them over 60 feet (18 m) high.

After two weeks, everything is ready for opening night. On this night, ice-skating and skiing contests are held. But most people come to enjoy the beautiful sculptures under the bright, colorful lights.

Getting ready for the fun

The city prepares for the festival two weeks ahead of time. Trucks dump huge loads of snow in the main square. Big blocks of ice are taken from the frozen river. A team of sculptors is assigned one area to work in. They use tools on the ice and snow just as if it were marble.

THINGS FOR YOU TO DO

Spring is a special time in Japan because it is cherry blossom season. Cherry blossoms begin to bloom in February on the southern island of Okinawa. In the next few months, they blossom all across the country, finally opening on the northern island, Hokkaido, in May. The blossoms only last for a week, so the Japanese fill the parks to enjoy the sight while it lasts. Here are two great activities to honor the cherry blossom festival.

Origami blossoms

Making *origami* [o-ree-GA-mee] blossoms is easy. You'll need 5-inch (12.5-cm) squares of pink and white tissue paper and 3-inch (7.5-cm) pieces of green wire.

Stack a few sheets of paper and fold them in half diagonally. Unfold the paper and re-fold into a rectangle. Fold once more in half to make a square. Unfold the paper completely.

Put the two diagonal corners together, and press in the sides along the creases. You should be holding a square now. Fold it in half to make a triangle.

Make a hook at one end of the wire and staple it to the corner of the folded paper. The fold should be at the right side. Cut the top of the paper into a semi-circle and make a fringe. Pull back each layer of paper. Now fluff the layers to make the flower full.

CHERRY BLOSSOMS

Cher - ry blooms, | cher - ry blooms, | Pale a - gainst the | bright spring sky,
Sa - ku - ra, | sa - ku - ra, | Ya - yo - i - no | so - ra - wa
sah - koo - rah | sah - koo - rah | yah - yoh - ee - noh | soh - rah - wah

Reach as far as | we can see, | Mi - sty blos - som | in a cloud, | Smell the per - fume
Mi - wa - ta - su | ka - gi - ri | Ka - su - mi - ka | ku - mo - ka | Ni - o - i - zo
mee - wah - tah - soo | kah - gee - ree | kah - soo - mee - kah | koo - moh - kah | nee - oh - ee - zoh

on the air. | Come with me, | come with me, | Come and see, | come and see.
i - zu - ru | I - za - ya, | i - za - ya, | Mi ni | yu kan.
ee - zoo - roo | ee - zah - yah | ee - zah - yah | mee - nee | you - kan

---

Things to look for in your library

The Boy of the Three-Year Nap. Allen Say and Dianne Snyder (Houghton Mifflin Co., 1988).
A Carp for Kimiko. Katherine Roundtree and Virginia Knoll (Charlesbridge Publications, 1993).
If I Lived in Japan. Roseanne Knorr (Longstreet Press, 1995).
The Japanese. (Agency for Instructional Technology).
Japanese Boy: The Story of Taro. (Encyclopaedia Britannica Educational Corporation).
Peach Boy. William H. Hooks (Gareth Stevens, 1996).
Postcards from Japan. Zoe Dawson (Raintree/Steck Vaughn, 1996).
The Samurai Warriors. Philip Steck (Kingfisher, 1994).

MAKE A DARUMA DOLL

The most common time to see a ***daruma*** [da-ROO-ma] doll is in late December. When they are sold, the dolls don't have eyes. That's because one eye is drawn in on New Year's Day when a wish is made. The other eye isn't drawn in until the wish comes true.

You will need:

1. Old newspapers
2. A flour and water paste
3. A balloon
4. Scissors
5. Tempera paints
6. Paintbrushes
7. A pencil or pen
8. A paint tray
9. Masking tape
10. Glue
11. Cardboard

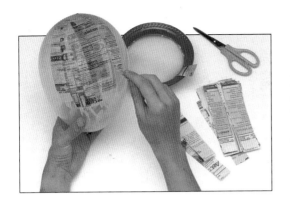

1 Blow up a round balloon until it's slightly smaller than your head. Using strips of newspaper and a flour and water paste, papier mâché the balloon until it is completely covered. Allow to dry.

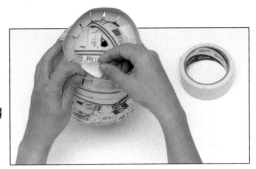

2 Cut a 2-inch (5-cm) strip from the cardboard. Make small cuts in the strip. Attach the two ends with masking tape. Turn in the cut sections. Glue the strip to the bottom of the balloon.

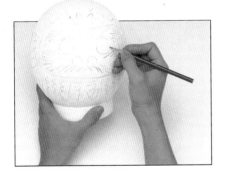

3 Using a pencil or pen, draw the face of the doll on the paper.

4 Now paint the doll using bright, festive colors, such as red and gold. Be sure not to paint in the eyes yet!

MAKE ONIGIRI

A favorite Japanese snack at festival time, or any time, is *onigiri* [o-NEE-gee-ree]. These delicious and healthy snacks are made from rice. Sometimes the rice is wrapped in seaweed. Other times it is covered with sesame seeds. You can put whatever you like inside, or follow our recipe and use sour plums.

You will need:
1. 1 cup (225 g) rice
2. 1¼ cups (300 ml) water
3. 3 sour plums
4. 1 sheet seaweed
5. Salt
6. A cutting board
7. A saucepan
8. A wooden spoon
9. A measuring cup
10. A knife
11. Scissors
12. A plate
13. ¼ cup (40 g) roasted sesame seeds

1 Put the rice in a saucepan with a tight-fitting lid and cover the rice with 1¼ cups water. Bring the water to a boil on maximum heat. Lower the heat when you see steam coming from the edge of the lid. Simmer rice for 12–13 minutes on low heat.

2 While the rice is cooking, make a slit in the plums with a knife and remove the pit from inside.

3 After the rice has cooled, pick up a handful and make a well in the middle. Put a sour plum inside, then dust damp hands with salt. Squeeze the rice to make a triangle. Be sure to close up the middle completely so the plum isn't showing. Repeat this step with the other two plums.

4 Cut the seaweed into strips. Now wrap the rice triangle in seaweed or coat with sesame seeds. Leave to cool. Onigiri is eaten hot or cold with the fingers.

GLOSSARY

Ainu, 4 — The early settlers of Japan.

chimaki, 10 — Good luck charms of straw wrapped in bamboo leaves.

daruma, 28 — A New Year's doll said to make wishes come true.

hakama, 12 — Formal dress for men.

hina, 15 — A special set of dolls collected for Girl's Day.

hoko, 8 — The Japanese word for halberd. Floats made for the Gion Festival.

kimono, 12 — Traditional Japanese dress.

onigiri, 30 — Snacks made from rice and seaweed or sesame seeds.

origami, 26 — Japanese paper folding.

palanquin, 21 — A box supported by poles and carried on the shoulders.

shogun, 20 — A military leader in 12th–19th century Japan.

yabusame, 23 — A contest that tests the skill of archers on horseback.

INDEX

Picture Credits
Richard l'Anson: 8 (top), 11 (bottom); Axiom Photographic Agency: 6; BES Stock: 8 (bottom), 12, 14 (top and bottom), 15, 18, 23 (bottom), 25; Jon Burbank: 3 (top), 7 (bottom); Haga Library: 19 (top), 19 (bottom); Hutchison Library: 9, 10, 11 (top), 23 (top); Image Bank: 3 (bottom), 4, 7 (top); Japan National Tourist Organization: 26, 28; Life File: 2, 16 (top and bottom), 17; PANA: 24; Photobank: 1, 5, 13, 20, 21 (top), 21 (bottom), 22